First World War
and Army of Occupation
War Diary
France, Belgium and Germany

52 DIVISION
Divisional Troops
413 Field Company Royal Engineers
1 April 1918 - 31 May 1919

WO95/2893/3

The Naval & Military Press Ltd
www.nmarchive.com
Published in association with The National Archives

Published by

The Naval & Military Press Ltd

Unit 10 Ridgewood Industrial Park,

Uckfield, East Sussex,

TN22 5QE England

Tel: +44 (0) 1825 749494

www.naval-military-press.com

www.nmarchive.com

This diary has been reprinted in facsimile from the original. Any imperfections are inevitably reproduced and the quality may fall short of modern type and cartographic standards.

© Crown Copyright
Images reproduced by permission of The National Archives, London, England, 2015.

Contents

Document type	Place/Title	Date From	Date To
Heading	WO95/2893-3		
Heading	52nd Division 413th (Lowland) Fld Coy R.E. Apr 1918-May 1919		
Heading	52nd Divisional Engineers 413th (Lowland) Field Company R.E. April 1918		
War Diary	Ludd	01/04/1918	01/04/1918
War Diary	Kantara	02/04/1918	02/04/1918
War Diary	Alexandria	03/04/1918	03/04/1918
War Diary	At Sea	04/04/1918	11/04/1918
War Diary	Marseilles	12/04/1918	14/04/1918
War Diary	Sailly Bray	17/04/1918	27/04/1918
War Diary	Aire	29/04/1918	30/04/1918
Heading	War Diary 413th (Lowland) Field Co R.E. From 1st May 1918 Till 31st May 1918 Vol IV No. 5		
Heading	War Diary 413th (Low) Field Co R.E. From 1st May 1918 Till 31st May 1918 Vol IV No.5		
War Diary	Aire	01/05/1918	05/05/1918
War Diary	St Eloy	06/05/1918	31/05/1918
Heading	War Diary For Month Of June 1918		
War Diary	St Eloy	01/06/1918	28/06/1918
Heading	War Diary For Month Of July		
War Diary	St Eloy	01/07/1918	18/07/1918
War Diary	Mont St Eloy	20/07/1918	21/07/1918
War Diary	Villers Au Bois	22/07/1918	22/07/1918
War Diary	Lozinghem	23/07/1918	29/07/1918
War Diary	Barlin	30/07/1918	30/07/1918
War Diary	Ecurie	31/07/1918	31/07/1918
Heading	War Diary For Month Of August 1918		
War Diary	Ecurie	01/08/1918	17/08/1918
War Diary	Bouvigny	18/08/1918	19/08/1918
War Diary	Agnez Duisance	20/08/1918	21/08/1918
War Diary	Bellacourt	22/08/1918	22/08/1918
War Diary	Grosville	23/08/1918	23/08/1918
War Diary	Ficheux	24/08/1918	24/08/1918
War Diary	Boisleux Au Mont	24/08/1918	24/08/1918
War Diary	Boisleux St Marc	24/08/1918	24/08/1918
War Diary	Boisleux St Marc	24/08/1918	27/08/1918
War Diary	Henin	27/08/1918	28/08/1918
War Diary	Boisleux Au Mont	28/08/1918	31/08/1918
Heading	War Diary 413th Lowland Field Coy R.E From 1st August 1918 Till 31st August 1918 Vol IV No.8		
Heading	War Diary For Month Ending Sept 1918 413th (Low) Field Co R.E Vol IV No.9		
War Diary	Henin Hill	01/09/1918	01/09/1918
War Diary	Bullecourt	02/09/1918	02/09/1918
War Diary	Queant	03/09/1918	04/09/1918
War Diary	Between Boyelles & Goisslles	05/09/1918	15/09/1918
War Diary	On Road Between Bullecourt & Quiant	15/09/1918	18/09/1918
War Diary	Longatte	19/09/1918	20/09/1918
War Diary	Pronville	24/09/1918	27/09/1918

War Diary	Moevres	27/09/1918	30/09/1918
Heading	War Diary 413th (Lowland) Field Co R.E Sept 1918 Vol IV No.9		
Heading	War Diary From 1st October To 31st October 1918 413th (Lowland) Field Co R.E Vol IV No.10		
War Diary	Cantaing	01/10/1918	05/10/1918
War Diary	Beaumetz	06/10/1918	07/10/1918
War Diary	Denier	08/10/1918	18/10/1918
War Diary	Mont St Eloi	19/10/1918	19/10/1918
War Diary	Henin Lietard	20/10/1918	20/10/1918
War Diary	Courcelles Les Lens	21/10/1918	30/10/1918
War Diary	Vieux Eglise	31/10/1918	31/10/1918
Heading	War Diary 413th (Low) Field Co R.E. 1st To 31st Oct 1918 Vol IV No.10		
Heading	War Diary From 1st To 30th Nov 1918 413 Fd Co R.E.		
War Diary	Vielle Iglise (Near St Amand)	01/11/1918	03/11/1918
War Diary	Cubray	04/11/1918	08/11/1918
War Diary	Hergnies	08/11/1918	09/11/1918
War Diary	Bruyere	10/11/1918	18/11/1918
War Diary	Ghlin	19/11/1918	21/11/1918
War Diary	Bruyere Masmey	22/11/1918	24/11/1918
War Diary	Masmey St Pierre	26/11/1918	30/11/1918
Heading	War Diary For Month Of December 1918		
War Diary	Masnuy St Pierre	01/12/1918	31/12/1918
Heading	413 Fd Coy R.E War Diary December 1918		
Heading	War Diary For Month Of January 1919		
War Diary	Masnuy St Pierre	01/01/1919	31/01/1919
Heading	War Diary For Month Of February 1919 413th Low Fld Coy R.E. Vol 11		
War Diary	Masnuy St Pierre	01/02/1919	22/02/1919
Heading	War Diary March 1919		
War Diary	Masnuy Saint Pierre	01/03/1919	21/03/1919
War Diary	Soignies	22/03/1919	31/03/1919
Heading	War Diary 413 Field Co R.E April 1919		
War Diary	Soignies	01/04/1919	30/04/1919
Heading	War Diary 413 Fd Co R.E Month Of April 1919 Vol V No.4		
Heading	War Diary For Month Of May 1919 413th Low Fld Coy R.E.		
War Diary	Soignies	01/05/1919	31/05/1919

Wool Again (3)

Wool/ 2 of 3 (3)

52ND DIVISION

413TH (LOWLAND) FLD COY R.E.

APR 1918 - MAY 1919

52nd Divisional Engineers

Disembarked MARSEILLES from EGYPT   12.4.18.

413th (Lowland) FIELD COMPANY R. E.

APRIL 1918.

Army Form C. 2118.

Instructions regarding War Diaries and Intelligence Summaries are contained in F. S. Regs., Part II. and the Staff Manual respectively. Title pages will be prepared in manuscript.

WAR DIARY
or
INTELLIGENCE SUMMARY.
(Erase heading not required.)

Place	Date	Hour	Summary of Events and Information	Remarks and references to Appendices
Ludd.	April 1918	1600	No 1 Section rigging the company without any tools to hand into No 2 Sec. The Pump Co by order of GHQ 608 gun. So that they could go on in tow. The whole company then entrained at Kantara and arriving there at 0800 and detained.	
Kantara	2		We had others had to hand in all horses, wagons except tool carts, harness and all native drivers and attached pioneer drivers sent to the Depot. Seven reinforcements joined us here. We entrained for Alexandria at 2100 over strength. Being 7 officers 214 other ranks and 8 tool carts.	
Alexandria	3		We arrived at Alexandria at 1000 and embarked on H.M.H.T. "Kingstonian" and lay in harbor all day.	
At Sea	4		We left Alexandria in company of H.M.T. Manitou at 1500 bound for Marseilles.	
	5.		Joined a convoy of about 20 ships from Port Said.	
	6 & 9		General Routine of ship. All men on deck at 0820 after breakfast, physical drill until 1/2 an hour before dinner 1230. dinner 1230. dinner kept clean of drill in afternoon. Boat drill 1100 until 1200. Rounds at 1020.	
	10.		S.S. Warwickshire Torpedoed, she was one of the convoy, the same night we went to ship's stations. We in the convoy was went on to England and we went to Coal Junkers. We left the convoy who was went on to Egypt. Torpedoes hit a coal bunker. We in Kingstonian left the convoy and was torpedoed on the port side. All men went at once to front stations. At 0505 The Kingstonian was torpedoed the engines were stopped on the way and put onto the boats. They should have been in pontoon lines and stopped on the way and put onto the boats had from told except 7 who were apparently slipped on the way, all other sappers had from told have been only 2 sappers Africans and 2 sappers missing were picked up by #H.M.S. Lychnis. The 7/6 2 officers and 2 sappers when picked up by a sloop which lay alongside our camp 19 to aft. The 7 other sappers were supposed to have been launched. At 0700 H.M.S. Lychnis tool carts and saved the sinking Kingstonian. No 1 & 2 were launched but the tool carts and along side and took the company. The orderly room was unable to but the Kingstonian was eventually beached men quarters it is believed was not submerged. The Kingstonian was eventually beached in Sardinia and all men picked up by the ship were put back on her. H.M.S. Lychnis and went full steam for Marseilles.	

Army Form C. 2118.

WAR DIARY
or
INTELLIGENCE SUMMARY.
(Erase heading not required.)

Instructions regarding War Diaries and Intelligence Summaries are contained in F. S. Regs., Part II. and the Staff Manual respectively. Title pages will be prepared in manuscript.

Place	Date 1918	Hour	Summary of Events and Information	Remarks and references to Appendices
Marseilles	April 12		Arrived at Marseilles at 0530 and disembarked at 0730. Company's strength was 7 Officers and 207 other ranks, all in hastily gathered up clothes and no boots or equipment of any sort. On the quay we were given shirts, socks, boots and tea and biscuits. And then marched off to No 8 Camp. On arrival here each man got 3 blankets, knife, fork, spoon, canteen and water bottle. Later they all got great coats and puttees and cap comforters. They were put into tents and given a hot meal.	
	14		Company entrained for Abbeville	
	17	1030	Early in morning we arrived at Abbeville, detained at 1030 marched to Grandvilliers. Then was taken up in motor lorries to Sailly Bray and were billeted there.	
Sailly Bray	18		Drew more clothing from Ordnance at Abbeville	
	19		Drew 13 light Draught Horses and 48 Flanders mules and mess cart	
	20		Drew Harness, steel helmets and bicycles	
	21-24		Training and drawing stores.	
	25		Gas lecture to whole Company. Drew equipment and ammunition	
	26		Drew remainder of horses and carts supply that drawing 85 limbers in lieu of G.S. carts	
	27		Drew some tools and box respirators.	
AIRE	29		Whole company marched to Noyelles and entrained there for AIRE where we arrived at 7200	
	30		Reconnaissance round country &c and reported on 13 rifle ranges	

K.K. Riffith Wilshire
Major R.E.
O.C. 413 (Cow) Field Coy, R.E.

Vol. 2

CONFIDENTIAL

WAR DIARY

413th (Lowland) Field Co. R.E.

from 1st May 1918
till 31st May 1918

Vol IV No 5

CONFIDENTIAL

WAR DIARY

413th (low) Field Co. R.E.

from 1st May 1918
till 31st May 1918

Vol IV No 5

Army Form C. 2118.

WAR DIARY
or
INTELLIGENCE SUMMARY
(Erase heading not required.)

Place	Date 1918	Hour	Summary of Events and Information	Remarks and references to Appendices
AIRE	May 1		Company in barracks at AIRE, training and re-equipping. One Physical Training Instructor from the Army Gymn Staff, 2 Bayonet fighting & 2 musketry instructors from the 157 Inf Brigade joined us. 157 Pioneer Company was reformed and reorganised with 2 officers and 100 other ranks, 155 and 156 Pioneer were also temporarily with the company until 410 & 412 Fld.Coys. could take them over.	
	2nd		Type of Sappers and Pioneers of the 4 companies training and we were re-equipping. Type of training done 0800 to 0900 Gas Drill. 0900 to 1000 Physical drill. 1000 to 1100 musketry. 1100 to 1200 Bayonet fighting 1400 to 1500 Musketry 1600 to 1600. Bayonet fighting 1600 to 1700 Physical training. The above was modified with an occasional Route March. On the afternoon of the 2nd however the 4 companies were put through Gas and cloud gas.	
	3 & 4		Company training as before also making targets and preparing ranges and bayonet fighting grounds for the infantry.	
	5		The transport started off by road for DIVISION. Advanced party of 3 officers and 6 other ranks went on to 10th Canadian Engineers Camp at St Eloy to make arrangements to take over their work.	
ST ELOY	6		Transport arrived by road at St Eloy and the sappers of the 413th Coy and Pioneers of 157 Coy arrived by train and were billeted for the night at farm near St Eloy. Advanced party of 1 officer and 5 O.R.s was sent on to 10th C.E.Coy. billets in front of Petit Vimy to make arrangements for taking over work next day. Pioneer Coys 155 & 156 were left behind at AIRE, to wait for 410 and 412 Fld.Coys. to take them over.	
	7		R.E. sections 1 & 2 and one officer went up to Petit Vimy 2 at a time arriving there by midday to relieve the 10th Canadians 2 sections who were working the line before. At 1830 an officer and section 3 & 4 of the Pioneers went up with the ration by road to the same place to act as a working party. At 2130 the remainder of the 2 companies and the transport went into camp vacated by the 10th Canadian Engineers, just north of St Eloy.	

WAR DIARY or INTELLIGENCE SUMMARY

Army Form C. 2118.

Place	Date 1918	Hour	Summary of Events and Information	Remarks and references to Appendices
S.T.E/04	May 8		Forward sections worked on trenches which consisted of putting in small shallow dugouts and finishing French drainage etc. Back sections half were employed on erecting another hut to accommodate the pioneers and half were on training. O.C. went up to forward billets.	
	9		2 pontoons and trestle taken to test Army Park at Ronchicourt and dumped. Lieut Thompson 1/5 H.L.I. joined the 157th Fd. Pioneers, to take command. 2/Lieut Penman returned to his battalion the following day.	
	10		Given blighty trench in front of Chaudière both sides of Lens Arras road to work in case of attack.	
	11		Started work on new Battalion H.Q. for left reserve battalion in ruined cellars of Vimy Village. Leave home started. First 2 men left on a fortnight's leave. Received 2 double tool carts & returned 2 G.S. limbers that were used as tool carts.	
	13		Got orders to hand over our forward dugouts to infantry. Moved out of old quarters. Could find no single group of dugouts to hold all the pioneer half company & Pioneers, therefore left one section brick stacks on section at foot of hill near Vimy, 2 sections on top of hill. Very unsatisfactory.	
	14		Asked for permission to dig other quarters in the Brown Line. Section 1 R.E. & Pioneer 3 went to rear H.Q. and section 3 R.E & Pioneer 1 came up to front quarters. On the 11th May an instructor was attached to the company to instruct two teams in the use of the Lewis Gun.	
	15		Lieut Rogerson went home on a fortnight's leave after an absence of nearly 3 years. Received our last 2 double tool carts & returned 2 G.S. limbers that were used as tool carts.	

Army Form C. 2118.

WAR DIARY
or
INTELLIGENCE SUMMARY.
(Erase heading not required.)

Instructions regarding War Diaries and Intelligence Summaries are contained in F.S. Regs., Part II. and the Staff Manual respectively. Title pages will be prepared in manuscript.

Place	Date 1918	Hour	Summary of Events and Information	Remarks and references to Appendices
St. E 69	May 16		Started repairs to Frazer Camp. Near Mt St Eloy.	
	17		Ordered to hand over all infantry Pioneers to a tunnelling Coy.	
	18		Above order cancelled for a day or two. Sent section 4 Pioneers & section 2 R.E. to run & get section 4 R.E. & section 2 pioneers up.	
	19		Ordered to hand all Pioneers over to Canadian Tunnelling Coy. for work on deep dugouts in Brown line & Vimy Battalion H.Q. 1 NCO & 7 sappers attached to 52nd Bns. M.G. Battalion to supervise works.	
	20		Started work on new Company HQ behind Green line.	
	21		Moved Section 3 back from forward post of Ridge to top of the lockRidge.	
	24		New forward company head quarters finished on top of Vimy Ridge by Humber Trench. Section 3 k.q. moved into them. 157 Inf Brigade changed with 155 Inf Brigade.	
	25		Section 3 came away from front line work. Company will section 1.	
	26		Lieut Dobbie went to Corps Gas School for a week's instruction.	
	27		155 Brigade want a new forward HQ about a mile behind their present place.	
	28		Work started on new Brigade HQ arranged HQ. 7 Elephants hut G Khe bastion.	
	29		Section 2 relieved Section 4.	
	30 & 31		Worked on Dugouts, prospecting doors painting & putting up notices, letting, putting up frames etc	

K.T.S.
Lt/Maj A.H. Williams
Major R.E.
4/3 (Lon) Field Co R.E.
31/5/18

SECRET

413 4th Cay Bde
9M 3

WAR DIARY
FOR MONTH OF JUNE 1918

WAR DIARY or INTELLIGENCE SUMMARY

Army Form C. 2118.

Place	Date 1918	Hour	Summary of Events and Information	Remarks and references to Appendices
St Eloy.	June 1		Sections Nºs 1 and 2 at forward position on VIMY RIDGE. Sections 3 & 4 at rear HQ. The sections on VIMY RIDGE were engaged on fitting gas proof curtains to dugouts. Camouflaging HUMBER C.T. Running the pumping engines for water supply, repairing duck tracks. The sections at Rear HQ were erecting elephant huts at Bde HQ.	
	3		Lieut Rogerson returned from Home Leave.	
	4		Section Nº 1 was relieved by Section Nº 3	
	5		Lieut James McL. had joined the company from the 552 A.T. Coy R.E. to take IC Lieut W.H.J. Wangford's place.	
	6		Lieut W.H.J. Wangford left the Company to join the 552 A.T. Coy R.E.	
	7		Commenced new work on camouflaging route from bottom of HUMBER C.T. to PEBBLE C.T. with a view to changing Brigades by daylight.	
	8		Nº 4 section relieved Nº 2 section	
	10		The screening of RED TRAIL was completed	
	11		156 Bnf Bde relieved the 155 Bnf Bde. A considerable part of this relief was done in daylight.	
	12		Communication trenches in front of Red & Brown lines to have Blocks, i.e. loop hole traverses with communication trench straightened for 40 yds.	
	14		Nº 1 section relieved Nº 3 section. Drew 2 remounts (Riders)	
	15		Lieut Kit from RMT Kingstonian tunnel up.	
	16-17		Works as usual. Fixing OLIVER Shrapnel proof sentry boxes in front line near deep dugout entrances.	

Army Form C. 2118.

WAR DIARY
or
INTELLIGENCE SUMMARY.
(Erase heading not required.)

Instructions regarding War Diaries and Intelligence Summaries are contained in F. S. Regs., Part II. and the Staff Manual respectively. Title pages will be prepared in manuscript.

Place	Date 1918	Hour	Summary of Events and Information	Remarks and references to Appendices
SE/109	June 18		No 4 Section on Vimy Ridge, was relieved by No 2 Section. Some rain in evening	
	19		Sent a sapper & 2 J.O. E 417 Coy RE Bours for instruction in Peter set for the electric lighting of Left Bde H.Q.	
	22		O.C. back from leave, took over work from Capt Bevenger who went on leave	
	24		No 3 Section on Vimy Ridge, was relieved by No 1 Section.	
	28		No 2 Section on Vimy Ridge was relieved by No 4 Section.	

K. B. Buffett Williams
Major RE
418 (Lowl) Field Coy RE
1/7/18

413 Fd Coy RE
1st A

SECRET

WAR DIARY
for
MONTH OF
JULY.

Volume IV

1-8-18

Army Form C. 2118.

WAR DIARY

(Erase heading not required.)

Instructions regarding War Diaries and Intelligence Summaries are contained in F. S. Regs., Part II. and the Staff Manual respectively. Title pages will be prepared in manuscript.

Place	Date 1918	Hour	Summary of Events and Information	Remarks and references to Appendices
St. Eloy	July 1		Disposition of the company as follows:- HQ company and sections 2 and 1 in rear camp near Buknall Farm. No 3 Pont S? Eloy, employed on work in rear camps and Battn area. Sections 3 & 4 were at forward HQ on Vimy Ridge, by Humb. French employed on putting in dugouts running pump engines to the front line water supply system, wiring, camouflage etc., graphing and general road upkeep works. The attached 157 By German Coy had the 2 & 4st Sections who were taken out of the Division were employed by the Canadian Tunnelling Company and head at the Buknall oaks at Za Chandin.	
	3		Defence of Vimy as a strong point on defense locality was proposed and plans for same started.	
	4		Section 3 went up to Vimy Ridge to relieve section 1 who came down to rest at Q. Lieut Rogerson and Sergt Campbell go to Rouen for an Engineering Course.	
	6			
	8		Section 2 relieved Section 4 at Vimy Ridge	
	9		Capt Kavanagh came back from afortnight home leave	
	11		Fine weather broke up and rain started	
	12		Lieut J.D. Dobbie went on a fortnights home leave.	
	13		Gashin's trunk a day so a premontation of anyhow was stopped owing Kinnall	
	14		Section 3 relieved section 1 on Vimy Ridge	
	15		Owing to a new change in disposition of the line and comes down to Listening. Of ares worked by the company, the right half of our sector was handed over to the 171 th Field C. RE. 155 Inf Brigade took over from 157 Inf Brigade. Work was started on 4 new posts halfway Black and Brown Lines. East part of Platoon	
	17			
	18		Got a warning order saying that Division would be relieved by the 7th & 20th Div so stopped the	

Army Form C. 2118.

WAR DIARY
or
INTELLIGENCE SUMMARY.
(Erase heading not required.)

Place	Date	Hour	Summary of Events and Information	Remarks and references to Appendices
Mont St Eloy	20		Sent to Ranchicourt for my pontoons and trestles.	
	21		O.C. 156th Field Co R.E. came to look over works.	
Villers au Bois	22		Handed works over to 156th Field Co R.E. and company moved off to Suburban camp at Villers au Bois.	
Lozinghem	23		Company moved to Lozinghem Village near Pernes. Transport by Road and Sappers by Train.	
	24 to 29		Company Training	
Barlin	30		Company moved by Road to Barlin dropping pontoons at Ranchicourt	
Ecurie	31		Company moved by Road to Madagascar Corner near Ecurie & relieved Canadian Engineers from the Line.	

J.R. Griffith Williams
Major R.E.
A.I.3.(2015) Field Co R.E.
1/8/18

CONFIDENTIAL.

WAR DIARY
FOR
MONTH OF
AUGUST 1918.

Army Form C. 2118.

WAR DIARY
or
INTELLIGENCE SUMMARY.
(Erase heading not required.)

Instructions regarding War Diaries and Intelligence Summaries are contained in F. S. Regs., Part II. and the Staff Manual respectively. Title pages will be prepared in manuscript.

Place	Date 1918	Hour	Summary of Events and Information	Remarks and references to Appendices
Ennis	August 1		Company took over works in left of A.B.F area and neighbourhood. Area HQ in farm railway alley by Bailleul village. Two alleyways Bideriod village.	
	2		Section 1 and HQ went forward to dugouts in a sunken road south of Bailleul and the railway embankment. HQ the house there and Section 2 & 3 went to Bideriod camp and Madagascar corner near Ennis village.	
	4		With the new area was counted north of drainage, chalk flooring and shelter for the men.	
			167 Pioneer Company was attached to this HQ Field Coy RE for works. We took charge of 5 demolition schemes in our own area and are in support area.	
	10.		Half the pioneer company was sent off to join the Tunnelling Company.	
	16.		The half the company trained was relieved by a section of the 13th Field Coy R.E. and came back to Relvad Camp.	
	17		Whole company was training and moved back. This was moved to Beuvigny and were billetted there.	
Beuvigny	18		Company moved by route march	
	19		Company trained	
Agnez Duisans	20		Whole company moved by route march to Agnez Duisans at night and were billetted in huts near by.	
	21		Company trained	
Bellacourt	22		Company moved by route march to Bellacourt and camped in the open.	
Grosville	23		Company moved to Grosville and billeted for the night	
Ficheux	24 5am		Company moved at 2 am to Ficheux and halted.	
Boisleux au Mont	10am		Company moved at 10 am to South of Boisleux au Mont	
Boisleux St Marc	2pm		Moved H.Q. and 4 sections with 1st Canta. to Boisleux St Marc. offlose lines behind Boisleux au Mont	

D. D. & L., London, E.C.
(A801) Wt. W17711/M2031 750,000 5/17 Sch. 52 Forms/C2118/14

WAR DIARY
or
INTELLIGENCE SUMMARY.

Army Form C. 2118.

Instructions regarding War Diaries and Intelligence Summaries are contained in F. S. Regs., Part II. and the Staff Manual respectively. Title pages will be prepared in manuscript.

(Erase heading not required.)

Place	Date 1918	Hour	Summary of Events and Information	Remarks and references to Appendices
Poixlaux &/Havr	Augt 24		Did water, and road reconnaissance and between villages of Poixlaux and Harant at race & Poing Taugeville and Havrin. Repaired roads between Poing Taugeville and Havrin at night.	
	25		Did Railway road and water reconnaissances. Repaired roads between the village and a bridge between Boixlaux station and Poing Taugeville. Section 3 went forward to put up 3 boards in Tandem "Fat Suited" and "Footer" and if necessary on getting more it was decided the blocks was not wanted. Its tanks being too small the dangerous. Roads between Havrin and these Tandems were repaired during the night.	
	26		Repaired Heavy bridge in Poing Taugeville over the Copal River. Put up 2 toughs by the river trento house. Repaired roads.	
	27	3pm	Brought up transport & camp at dag back and prepared to move forward. Moved into a new camp N.E. of Havrin at 3 p.m. Built 3 men troughs when gunner horse lines seemed thickest Repaired roads forward and a bit of Havrin at Night reconnoitred the sunken river near Fontaine le Guizelle.	
Havrin	28	3 a.m.	Moved back to our old horse lines near Poixlaux on trent leaving Section 2 to 176 Field Coy RE.	
Below our tent.	29		hard evacuate, and amusements. They rejoined us that evening.	
	30		Company training.	
	31		to Company repairing roads on Havrin Hill. Section 1 took our water arrangements from 51st Field Co RE. Section 1th building new Div HQ not near Cironelle	

W.S. Griffith Williams
Major R.E.
1/9/18
M.S. (Act.) Fld Co R.E.

CONFIDENTIAL

WAR DIARY.

413th Lowland
Field Coy RE

From 1st August 1918
till 31st August 1918

Vol IV N°8

Vol 6

52nd Dr

CONFIDENTIAL

War Diary
For
Month Ending
Sept. 1918.

413th (Low) Field Co RE

Vol IV No 9

Volume V.
1/10/18

WAR DIARY
or
INTELLIGENCE SUMMARY

Army Form C. 2118.

(Erase heading not required.)

Instructions regarding War Diaries and Intelligence Summaries are contained in F.S. Regs., Part II. and the Staff Manual respectively. Title pages will be prepared in manuscript.

Place	Date 1918	Hour	Summary of Events and Information	Remarks and references to Appendices
Hénin-Hill	1		Head quarter section and Section 2 moved to a new camp in Summit. Trench on Hénin Hill leaving the Pontoons and Tools and Section 1 in the old camp. Sections 3 & 4 were building Divisional H.Q. Section 4 joined us on Hénin Hill late on that night.	
Bullecourt	2		Moved camp to top of hill halfway between Croisilles and Bullecourt. Sections 1 and 3 joined us here.	
Quéant	3		Moved camp to Quéant where Pontoons etc joined me and developed water in the latter. Worked on roads in Quéant and Pronville.	
	4		Repairing roads in Quéant and developed water in Pronville.	
	5		Moved back to Divisional H.Q. Sunday. Pontoons back to old camp. Self took enlarging Divisional H.Q. for a Corps H.Q.	
	6		Working on Corps H.Q.	
	7-10		Working on Corps H.Q. with section, rest of one section every day, a foreman	
	11-14		Working on Corps H.Q. and ? hostings ? with section to work at (?'s) Brig H.Q. Off N°2 section to work at (?'s) Brig H.Q.	
Mt Between Bullecourt & Quéant	15		Off N°2 section had a day off. Company had a rest up & take over from 505 Field Co RE at a camp between Bullecourt and Quéant. Section 3 to take over work in gas hosting dugouts. Section 4 to take over watering arrangements.	
	16		Remainder of company followed in the afternoon.	

WAR DIARY
or
INTELLIGENCE SUMMARY.
(Erase heading not required.)

Army Form C. 2118.

Place	Date 1918	Hour	Summary of Events and Information	Remarks and references to Appendices
Between Quéant & Pronville	Sept (?)		Handed over all works taken over from 103 Fd Co R.E. & 410 Fd S R.E. except gas blanketing. ½ Section 1 moved up to the Canal du Nord in the afternoon being live to do gas blanketing. ½ Section 2 were attached to Infantry battalions for work. ½ Section 1 to Baralle for working dugouts.	
	18		½ Section went on to Baralle. Railway job cancelled.	
Longatte	19		Handed over to the Canadians and moved back to Longatte.	
	20		Sections 1 and 3 handed over their FdSp equipments Consolidated Morres. Trestles were sent for to be ready for crossing the Canal du Nord to supplement the existing crossings.	
Pronville	24		Shifted camp forward again to neighbourhood S.W. of Pronville in sunken bank line. Section 3 rejoined me from 412 Field R.E. Section 4 employed road widening.	
	25-6		Section 1 reported me from 412 Field R.E. Brigade formed HQrs at Tadpole Copse. Section 2 employed in making 2 Brigade forward HQrs at Inchy.	
	26		Made Tank Saddles and finished making & Old lestis tracks just before zero am. Nord pontoons and approaches.	
	27		Moved company forward through Inchy-Quesnoit line to point of proposed company HQ at 11.30 am to prepare route forward through Moeuvres to chosen site of proposed 6 track bridge site over Canal du Nord. Found Inchy though his not yet cleared of enemy machine gunners wounded casualties 6. At 10.30 am. Had Tank bridge [illegible] and approach scale land pieces bridge ready at 6 0 p.m. Company camped S.W. of Moeuvres.	
Moeuvres	29		Disarmed tank bridge and sent all bridging material forward at 6.15 = On exit to night to company standing ready to move forward.	
	30			

1 C/P E A H Williams
Major R.E.
413 (Lon) Field Co R.E.

2/10/18

52nd

Confidential

War diary

413th (Lowland)
Field Co RE

Septr. 1918

Vol IV No 9

SECRET.
ORIGINAL. COPY.

No 7

WAR DIARY

FROM

1st OCTOBER TO 31st OCTOBER. 1918.

413th (Lowland) Field Coy RE

Vol IV No 10

WAR DIARY or INTELLIGENCE SUMMARY

Army Form C. 2118.

Place	Date 1918	Hour	Summary of Events and Information	Remarks and references to Appendices
Canting	Oct 1		The whole company lay in the morning, moved camped about a mile S.E. of Moeuvres. Orders to move forward were received early in the morning and company moved at 10.10 a.m. to Canting camping in trenches not south of the west end of Canting and found by early to assist 157 Inf. Bde of battle. Transport complete with M.L. of Brain court.	
	2		Received orders to take over all bridge and water points on the Escaut River and St Quenton Canal from 412 Field Company and R more company. Rtts Bat and S of Canting village. Move in dugouts and cellars.	
	3		Section 1 put up a footbridge over the river of felled trees and planting. Section 2 was in charge of ridge maintenance and provided loading parties. Section 3 reconnoitred for bridge apparatus and worked at water point. Section 4 was in charge of Section 1 put up a Bailon trail bridge over river Escaut. Section 2 replaced a sunken pontoon in Pontoon bridge. Lost 2 man killed & 6 wounded.	
	4		Got orders late at night & land over to 58 Div Engs.	
Beaumetz	5		Company moved out of Canting and camped near Beaumetz.	
	6		Company has transport entrance to Petit Moeuvres. Transport went by road.	
Deniet	7		Company by train and road arrived at Deniecourt and billeted there.	
	8		Company by train and 1 section on works for brigade. Ranges etc	
	9 & 12		3 Sections training and 1 section on the ranges.	
	13		Whole company shooting on the ranges.	
	14		Company had a day off for sports	
	15		3 Sections training and 1 on works	
	16 & 16		2 Sections training and 2 on works	

WAR DIARY or INTELLIGENCE SUMMARY

Army Form C. 2118.

Instructions regarding War Diaries and Intelligence Summaries are contained in F. S. Regs., Part II. and the Staff Manual respectively. Title pages will be prepared in manuscript.

(Erase heading not required.)

Place	Date	Hour	Summary of Events and Information	Remarks and references to Appendices
Mont St Eloi	19		Whole company marched to Mont St Eloi and camped for the night	
Hem Lietard	20		Le Ponds Camp. The company marched to Hemin Lietard and were billeted there	
Bully Grenay	21		The company moved early to Grenclas by lorry to take over work from 1st Siege Coy RAH RE. They were just starting to erect 4 Hopkins Girder Bridges and had got the concrete piers but had had an accident with 2 of the top plates which made completion of the Superstructure of 2 bridges impossible	
	22		Our company and 25 tons of wood wagons and loaded out tarpaulins, picks & crowbars and dug brick foundation biers for and string up of dumpy level behind the brick pier of the Tent Town in this greatly levelling undulations by means level and banging rods. Laid and levelled two tons mortar in preparation of the beams and they not until 2 days by lack of just plates which did not arrive until next stay. Groove & plate arrived and beams were concreted up and diagonals placed in position. All but most work over 4 no. army & Whitland and trestle.	
	23			
	24			
	25		CG of the Table arrived and diagonals were raised up. 4 In manu etapi CG of the Table arrived let in staff timen, was carried for the remaining tackle around by candle light. Work until 10 pm by candle light	
	26		Derricks were erected and top beams built on and all was	
	27		had having and launching over harnesses put on and all was vacated. Launching team who site was ordered to remove the launching	

WAR DIARY
INTELLIGENCE SUMMARY

Army Form C. 2118.

Place	Date	Hour	Summary of Events and Information	Remarks and references to Appendices
	26		Tackle. After it was worked on all night and was nearly by [?] day. Owing to the nearness of the launching end it [?] and after it was to shift & haul up [?] in our heavy [?] To we [?] forward what had to be taken off when the [?] was nearly half launched and in pieces being put on to lengthen the [?] tackle when the [?] was all on except one long [?]. Launching commenced at 12 noon and though moving at a rate of 1 foot a minute was not across until 6pm. owing to the close meshes [?] through this quarter of an hour spent on the [?] to the body on the launching side was then jacked down on its [?] bed and it was found that the length was 6" over. Another [?] was brought back [?] the land was 1½" out of [?], due to the rough methods used. Work continued all night on the flooring. [?] was open for traffic by midnight.	
	27th	0730	First heavy guns went over. A tractor + 8" howitz. and carriage defeated the bridge, too low then 1" [?]. T. Co. side walks were put on and the bridge was complete at 6pm.	
Vieux Eglise	28st		Company moved back to the Division and billeted Vieux Eglise	

KB 6th A Williams
Major RE
413 RE

1/11/18

CONFIDENTIAL

WAR DIARY

413th (Lond) Field
Co. R.E.

1st to 31st Dec. 1918.

Vol. IV No. 10

SECRET.

War Diary
From
1st to 30th Nov. 1918.

413 Fd Co. R.E.

Army Form C. 2118.

WAR DIARY
or
INTELLIGENCE SUMMARY.
(Erase heading not required.)

Instructions regarding War Diaries and Intelligence Summaries are contained in F. S. Regs., Part II. and the Staff Manual respectively. Title pages will be prepared in manuscript.

Place	Date 1918	Hour	Summary of Events and Information	Remarks and references to Appendices
Vieille Eglise (near Solesmes)	Nov 1		Company standing by. Have reconnoitred to Lecelles	
	2		Company engaged in clearing carts and repairing the road bridges reconnoitring Pontains and Pontoon sites and took 6 equipment. Collecting material for 2 RPA bridges and took over civilian area the canal and work near Thun. Handed over all work to the 2105th (Lond) Field Coy RE at night	
	3			
CURRAY	4		Took over all work from 158th Field Coy RE and moved whole company to Curral.	
	5		Got let spring bath working for the 159 ht brigade and started collecting Jerusalem Rafts and sending them forward.	
	6		Finding work on Jerusalem Rafts and sending them forward.	
	7		Ditto	
	8		Got orders to close the retreating Germans Section 3 put 4 light Jerusalem raft bridge over the canal and River at Odomez and Section 1,2&4 collected and put over 2 pontoon bridge at Hergnies Whole company moved to Hergnies for the night	
Hergnies	9		Took up the 4 light bridge and sent 1,2 rafts forward with Section 1 maintained 4 Pontoon bridge	
Bruges	10		Moved forward to Brunges	
	11th		Bursting and heavy held bridge over the canal at Stambrages	
	12		Traffic handed over 4CA at Espain	

Army Form C. 2118.

WAR DIARY
or
INTELLIGENCE SUMMARY.
(Erase heading not required.)

Instructions regarding War Diaries and Intelligence Summaries are contained in F. S. Regs., Part II. and the Staff Manual respectively. Title pages will be prepared in manuscript.

Place	Date	Hour	Summary of Events and Information	Remarks and references to Appendices
Aurigne Ethin	18th Feb		Finishing Trenches to the huts and stuff.	
	19		Whole company marched to Ethin	
	20		Drill and cart cleaning	
	21		Ditto	
Aurigne Masny station	22		Whole company marched to Hugo Masny station	
	23 & 24		Drill and Cart cleaning	
Masny St Pierre	26		Whole company marched to Masny St Pierre	
	27		Whole company was expected in full marching order by GOC	
	28		Drill and cart cleaning	
	29		Ditto	
	30		[illegible]	

W/S Griffith Williams
Major RE
W 3 Kesland Cello RE

413th Coy R.E.

War Diary
for
Month of December
1918

Army Form C. 2118.

WAR DIARY
or
INTELLIGENCE SUMMARY.
(Erase heading not required.)

Instructions regarding War Diaries and Intelligence Summaries are contained in F. S. Regs., Part II. and the Staff Manual respectively. Title pages will be prepared in manuscript.

Place	Date	Hour	Summary of Events and Information	Remarks and references to Appendices
MASNY ST PIERRE	DEC.1918 1.		Company paraded in marching order. Pt 9 Lewis Gun Sections collected by Army workshops. Head of men employed on fatigue party of 15.	
	2.		The Company Drill & Musketry. Lectures by Section Commanders & NCOs & Musketry on Lewis Gun	
	3.		Pts 2 & 4 Lewis Guns at their Coys. Command to cart material from Manso station to MASNY. 57 Pieces for River Infirmary. 6 Lewis Gun teams for Cadre School. 6 German Maxim employed.	
	4.		Company Route March. Lectures eleven applied. Wireless Practice. Manoeuvres commenced.	
	5.		School on Sanitation on Baths & Improvements Dress in ordinary commenced.	
	6.		No 1 Salvage Party to WARDISE. Work commenced on Rifle Range at W24 C02 – X 15 ct CEUPAL – Ref 40000 SHEET 52 35.2.5/1.44 Infantry working parties employed on same.	
	7.		Divine Education Lecture on Care of Rifle & Rifle Equipment Cartring matinee from Divn Lewis Gun	

WAR DIARY
or
INTELLIGENCE SUMMARY.
(Erase heading not required.)

Army Form C. 2118.

Place	Date Dec 18	Hour	Summary of Events and Information	Remarks and references to Appendices
MASNUY ST PIERRE	8		Parade inspection and kit inspection. Roll call Service on Sports ground. R.C. Church Service 9/15	
	9		Drill & Education. Works - making latrine seats. Baths & Games - nature of work from items as shewn.	
	10		S.G. men found to replace men sent to P. groups wet weather to field ambulance & horse lines. Bde Entertainment Review Cin. Runners concert meetee in Bridge Brummell Divce & Education works (Bridge Brummell) Divce & Education	
	11		I.C. Bde Gym Inions Gen school Hawks Roc - Ouvhorks Educ out & Ranges. Works for 29.99. Bdg ret. to Entre rests to ceremonial. Remounted Gun wagons.	
	12		Divce & Education - Works - H.Q.R. & 137 Bygne Bde Brummells	
	13		Ditto.	
	14		Ditto.	

Army Form C. 2118.

WAR DIARY
or
INTELLIGENCE SUMMARY.
(Erase heading not required.)

Instructions regarding War Diaries and Intelligence Summaries are contained in F. S. Regs., Part II. and the Staff Manual respectively. Title pages will be prepared in manuscript.

Place	Date	Hour	Summary of Events and Information	Remarks and references to Appendices
MAGNY ST PIERRE	Dec 1918 15		Church Parade.	
	16		Drill - Works:- Billet improvements were carried out & H.Q. Left Wing of the Battalion's Billets. Improvements.	
	17		Company Inspected by O.C. 52nd Division	
	18		Drill, Education. Works:- Billet improvements for Bynes. Care is being taken for spring cleaning, sign writing, inventory " " "	
	19		Drill, Education, Works. - Billet improvements for 157 Brigade	
	20		Works & Education	
	21		Ditto	
	22		Company had a day off and a church parade	
	23 & 24		Works & Education	
	25		Xmas day Works & games	
	26 & 27		Works & Education	
	28		Raining hard all day. Works & Education	
	29		Company had a day off	

[signature]

Army Form C. 2118.

WAR DIARY
or
INTELLIGENCE SUMMARY.

(Erase heading not required.)

Instructions regarding War Diaries and Intelligence Summaries are contained in F. S. Regs., Part II, and the Staff Manual respectively. Title pages will be prepared in manuscript.

Place	Date	Hour	Summary of Events and Information	Remarks and references to Appendices
Boske & Etrueton	30			
	31		½ en hours General Drill, Works and Education	

H. G. Griffith Williams
Major RE
413 (Lons) Field Coy RE
2/11/18

H Bolt
Coy RE
War Diary
December
1916

SECRET

413 Fd Coy R.E. Vol 10

WAR DIARY.
FOR
MONTH OF JANUARY
1919.

Volume I   1-2-19

WAR DIARY or INTELLIGENCE SUMMARY

Army Form C. 2118.

Masnil St. Pierre

Place	Date 1919	Hour	Summary of Events and Information	Remarks and references to Appendices
	1.		The whole company was billeted in Masny St. Pierre engaged in Billet improvement, Education, Training and recreation. Strength of Company on this date was as follows:- 7 Officers, 203 OR's, and 70 horses and mules. 2 horses and 1 hot hanging total down R.E. Reminds.	
	2.		Company had the day off to game etc. Company had ½ an hour ceremonial drill in the morning and were then dismissed to Educational classes and works until 1600. Education in France 2 men attended. 10 men of the mounted section were detailed for Transport jobs etc. 1 Field wagon and 2 RE limbers were used for Transport jobs etc. At Noon were told to report R.110 & Field 8, RE in duty reducing officers Strength to 6 officers. Company did ½ an hour ceremonial drill and were then dismissed Education and works Training Education:- 0930 to 1020 Building 10 men of N°3 Section were detailed for recreational Training. Construction attached 1030 to 1130 Practical Maths at which 1 attended. One man retired from hospital who had been sick & strength hanging total Strength 7 OR & 204. Transport Numbers.	
	3.		Whole company was medically inspected by M.O. for scabies and bies and found clean. The company was for own baths. 10 men from Section 4 were detailed for recreational Training. Education 0930 to 1020 Mechanique at which 6 attended Distribution of company on this date as follows:- Leave to U.K. 10, OR Orderly at Div. HQ ½ pipale 1. OR attached 416 F.W6yRE 1 Offer attached ½ HE 1 2. OR 56th Inf. Brg. 2. OR Leave in France 1. OR " ½ HE 1 2. " Railway 1. " Hospital 1. OR " ½ HE 1 2. " Electricity 1. " attached 52 Div H.Q 1. OR " ½ HE 1 2. " Remainby 6. 169 " Engaged " Rein Sys 3. O.R. " Batt'y Transport 1. " On States on 1st S had attached " H.Q R.E 5. O.R " ½ L.F Amb 1. " Medical Officer, 1 B.Sc Officer, 1 Pioneer officer and 18 infantry men on carpenting tinsmith and painting courses.	

Jan uary

WAR DIARY or INTELLIGENCE SUMMARY

Army Form C. 2118.

Place: Masney St Pierre
Date: 1919 January

Date	Hour	Summary of Events and Information	Remarks
5th		Company had the day off. 1 mule broke away from hus and was shot.	
6th		Company marched to Sendine to attend 153rd Inf Brigade ceremonial parade of its distribution of medal ribbons. Transported 1 Tech wagon and 2 RE limbers.	
7th		Company marched to Anctove in drill order. Transported 1 Tech wagon and 2 RE limbers.	
8th		Company carried on the usual billet improvement works and alterations. 0915 RTO's Mechanics attended. 6 attended.	
9th		Works as usual. Transport 2 RE limbers & phaeton 0915 RTO's Band attendance 6. Lt Darby the C.S.M and a sapper proceeded to UK for demobilization. 2 NCO's and a driver fought mounted section also proceeded RUK for demobilization. Sapper Quig injured at Football and admitted to hospital. 0915 RTO's Building Construction attendance 21	
10th		Works as usual. Transport 3 limbers Education 0915 RTO's Building Construction attendance that to hospital. Lieut McNab thrown off horse and hurt	
11th		Works as usual. Transport 2 limbers	
12th		Company had a day off. 1 Sergt and 8 sappers proceeded to UK for demobilization. 3 sappers & three dismobility sappers proceeded to company as reinforcements	
13th		Works as usual Transport 1 tech wagon and 6 horses hut sections and skeleton gates.	
14th		Works as usual. All men had 170 Steadies for examination and Maths attendance 4 Maths attendance 16 1015 RTO's Building Construction attendance 16 1015 RTO's Education 0915 RTO's Building Construction 2 sappers proceeded RUK for demobilization. 2 Sappers proceeded to UK for demobilization	
15th		Works as usual 7 horses had RE workcare 2 Sappers proceeded to 6 horses hurt & civilians	
16th		Works as usual 2 limbers used to company transport and has and fired clean. Works carried on as usual 01 170 to earthen and brought them over. 1 horses left	
17th		Whole company was inspected up 153 Great pants and brought them over. 1 horses left ft Transport 2 tech wagons picked up 153 Building Contractor attendance 13. 10'15 RTO's Maths Civilians Education attendance 4	

Army Form C. 2118.

WAR DIARY
or
INTELLIGENCE SUMMARY
(Erase heading not required.)

Place: Masnuy St Pierre

Date 1919	Hour	Summary of Events and Information	Remarks and references to Appendices
January 18.		Whole company paraded in great coats and drill order for a devisional ceremonial parade on promotion by the Corps commander. Company strength on this date was as follows:— 7 officers 187 other ranks 67 horses and mules. They were distributed as follows:— Leave to UK. 1 Officer 8 OR attached 1/6 HLI — 1 OR Electric Pws — 1 OR; " in France 3 " — " 1/5 HLI — 2 " Corps Workshops — 1 "; Hospital — 1 " — " 1/2 LFA — 1 " C/C/S — 1 "; attached 51st Div HQ 1 " — " 56th RFA — 2 " Sappers remaining 78 " 7 oth M.T. SRP; " Div Sigs 3 " — " 2nd DAC — 3 " Drivers 45 "; " HQ RE 1 " — " Brass Py — 1 "; " 155th Bde HQ 4 " — " A10 RE 1 Officer 1 "; " 1/7 HLI 2 " — " Railway Coys —	
19.		Company had a day off	
20.		Company had a day off for the Div RE Sports 2 sappers demobilised	
21.		Works as usual	
22.		Works as usual. LT. McNAE rejoined Coy from Hospital. LT MITCHELL reported to HQ.R.E. as act a/c	
23.		Company went to Waterloo by Lorry	
24.		Works as usual	
25.		Started work on XXII Corps Race Course 5 sappers + 2 Drivers demobilised	
26.		Church Parade and one lorry load of men went to Waterloo.	
27.		Works on Race Course and Workshops	
28.		Works as usual	
29.		Works as usual 5 Sappers and 4 drivers demobilised	

WAR DIARY

or INTELLIGENCE SUMMARY

Army Form C. 2118.

(Erase heading not required.)

Instructions regarding War Diaries and Intelligence Summaries are contained in F. S. Regs., Part II. and the Staff Manual respectively. Title pages will be prepared in manuscript.

Place	Date 1919	Hour	Summary of Events and Information	Remarks and references to Appendices
	Jan 30		Notes as usual. Daily guard reduced by 1 man.	
	31		Works as usual. 24 hour guard reduced to 1 night n.c.o. with platoon during day. Company strength on this date was as follows:— 7 Officers 164 OR. 67 animals distributed as follows:—	

```
          O.R.
Leave to U.K.        1    9
Attached to R.E.     1    -
"  Div. Sig.         -    4
"  Div. WAVE         1    4
"  155th A.T.O.      -    3
"  58th R.F.A.       -    1
"  220 MSC           -    2
Ordinary Course Sick -    1
XXII Corps Workshop  -    -
Attached to F.U Coy RE  1  108
                     4    35
                          7-164
                            35
```

Officers of Company
Mooring
At Rouen } Drivers
5th Pers

W.S. Griffith Williams
Major R.E.
113 (Lowland) Fld Coy R.E.

SECRET

War Diary for
     Month of February 1919.

413th Low Fld Coy R.E.

WAR DIARY or INTELLIGENCE SUMMARY

Army Form C. 2118.

(Erase heading not required.)

Place: Masnuy St. Pierre

Date 1919	Hour	Summary of Events and Information	Remarks and references to Appendices
Feb 1		Strength 7 Officers 154 ORs 67 animals	
		Work on XXI Corps Race Course was the principal work of the company during the whole month.	
Feb 3		Demolished 4 drives and 3 sappers	
4		Demolished 8 sappers	
		No more left the company; work carried on the race course.	
6		Demolished 5 sappers	
7		Demolished 7 sappers	
8		Strength 7 Officers 127 ORs 67 animals 1 Officer 11 sappers demobilised	
9		Demolished 8 sappers	
10		Demolished 7 sappers	
11/12		Work on Race Course	
13		Demolished 1 Officer & 8 sappers and 14 horses	
14		Demolished 1 driver & 1 sapper	
15		Demolished 4 sappers & 2 horses	
21		Demolished 2 drivers & 6 horses	

K.B. Goff
Major A.W.
OC 3 London 1 Field Co.

4'? Fld Amb
Feb 12

CONFIDENTIAL

WAR DIARY.

MARCH
1919.

Army Form C. 2118.

WAR DIARY
or
INTELLIGENCE SUMMARY.

(Erase heading not required.)

Place	Date 1919 March	Hour	Summary of Events and Information	Remarks and references to Appendices
Masnuy Saint Pierre	1		Strength 51 Company 5 Officers 74 O.R. 57 horses and mules. Company went to Rivivak by lorry. 2 O.R. demobilized.	
	2.			
	3.		Company took down Grand Stand on XXII Corps Race course and when down received notice to remove stakes etc. 10% work on Race course recommenced and a mess pump was made.	
	5.			
	6.		Company employed on Race course.	
	7.		Grand Stand was re-erected Race course.	
	8.		Fourteen link on Stand and work on drains on Race course Strut etc during preceding week. 9 animals were	
	9.		All ammunition was handed in and work on Race course was proceeded with.	
	10.		XXII Corps Race meeting. Coy company employed on repairs to jumps etc.	
	12.		Company dismantled the Grand Stand and returned equipment.	
	13.		Cleared Trade equipment and loaded teals and pontoons onto wagons preparatory to a move to Sogries.	
	14.		Company was moderately inspected.	
	15.		Sortey & Checking Stores	
	16.		No parade. 5 more animal struck off strength during preceding week and 1 O.R. transferred to R.H.A R.E.	
	17 M6		Checking (sorting) Stores	
	19		Dismantled a Nissen hut at ERBISOUEL. 11 O.R. Demobilized	
	20 /521		8 O.R. posted to the 90th Field Coy R.E. on its Return. Checking & sorting Stores.	

Army Form C. 2118.

WAR DIARY
or
INTELLIGENCE SUMMARY.
(Erase heading not required.)

Instructions regarding War Diaries and Intelligence Summaries are contained in F. S. Regs., Part II. and the Staff Manual respectively. Title pages will be prepared in manuscript.

Place	Date 1919	Hour	Summary of Events and Information	Remarks and references to Appendices
	March 22		Company moved by march route to Sargnies. Horses being provided by the RFA and Lorries taking company kurms and Pantons and stages wagons. Company strength on this date 3 Officers, 54 OR and 11 animals. 18 men being transferred to HQRE and 1 demobilized.	
	23		Sorting and packing saddlery and staff. Shoeing up every 2 times.	
	24		Remaining 11 animals struck off strength.	
	25		Sorting and packing stores.	
	26		The last demobilizable men were demobilised and an officer transferred to 532 A.T. Coy R.E. Coy Stores and equipment examined by D.A.D.S and MG 1028's signed by him and MG 1028's old Div HQ to demount & engine teams. Party went to Dir HQ to demount & engine teams.	
	27		Work on repair to horse damaged by fire.	
	28		Repairing damaged saddlery and making ramps for loading animals onto train.	
	29		No Parade.	
	30		Making loading platform.	
	31		Company strength 2 Officers 53 OR and no animals	

W.G.H. William
Major RE
513 Lowland Field Coy RE.

CONFIDENTIAL

Vol 13

War Diary
413 Field Co. RE
April 1919

WAR DIARY
or
INTELLIGENCE SUMMARY.

(Erase heading not required.)

Army Form C. 2118.

Place	Date 1919	Hour	Summary of Events and Information	Remarks and references to Appendices
S	April 1		Cadre employed on making bedding ramps and gave up all explosives returning them to Sovrain	
	2		Cadre Rested	
	3rd to 6		Cadre employed on making bedding ramps etc	
S	7		Church voluntary and cadre were payed	
D	8		2 Carpenters reported to and C.R.E. made packing cases. Packed limbers wagons and part pontoon, made stencils	
I			Took remainder of carts to cargo park and cleaned & packed	
U			horses & cleaned carts	
O	9		Obtained 12 x 1/4 planking for making of packing cases	
	10 to 12		Cleaned horses and carts and made packing cases	
S	13		Church service. Voluntary	
	14		Box making, horses cleaning and packing and Whitewasher old wall damaged by previous Payed the cadre.	
	15		Cadre Rested	
	16		Rifle inspection	
	17		Box making and wall repairs	
	18		Ditto	

Army Form C. 2118.

WAR DIARY
or
INTELLIGENCE SUMMARY.
(Erase heading not required.)

Instructions regarding War Diaries and Intelligence Summaries are contained in F. S. Regs., Part II. and the Staff Manual respectively. Title pages will be prepared in manuscript.

Place	Date	Hour	Summary of Events and Information	Remarks and references to Appendices
	April 1919 19		Got all carts and wagons out except presuming of church voluntary	
	20		D.H.Q. proclaimed a holiday until	
	22	0900 on 22nd		
	24		Collecting and stacking R.E. Dump materials	
	25		Cart cleaning	
	26		Painting and stacking tent and boxes. Carting ramps & letters & painting wagons and mules	
	27		Nor service church voluntary	
	28		Pay parade	
	29		Painting wagons, repairing pont ports &c	
	30		Painting wagons and drawn train wagon	
			Painting wagon & cleaning train wagon	

G H d Williams
Major R.E.
213 (London) Fd Co. R.E.

CONFIDENTIAL

WAR DIARY
413 Fd Co RE

MONTH OF
APRIL 1919

VOL V
Nº 1

WAR DIARY
FOR MONTH OF
MAY 1919.
415th LOW. F.D. COY. R.E.

Army Form C. 2118.

WAR DIARY
or
INTELLIGENCE SUMMARY.
(Erase heading not required.)

Instructions regarding War Diaries and Intelligence Summaries are contained in F. S. Regs., Part II. and the Staff Manual respectively. Title pages will be prepared in manuscript.

Place	Date MAY 1919	Hour	Summary of Events and Information	Remarks and references to Appendices
SOIGNIES	1.		Coas employer Carpentering	
	2.		Rifle inspection	
	3.		Carpentering ditto	
	4.		Church Service voluntary case Prev.	
	5 to 9		Coas employer Carpentery & Box making	
	10.		Came hor aholiday Carpentery 11 men demoticed	
	11.		Church Service voluntary	
	12.		Carpentery	
	14.		Pay Parade	
	16.		Inocolary examiner	
	18.		Church Service voluntary	
	20.		Men have canteen money.	
	21.		Clean arms inspection	
			Pay Parade.	
	23.		Case Battea.	
	25.		Church Parade	

Army Form C. 2118.

WAR DIARY
or
INTELLIGENCE SUMMARY.
(Erase heading not required.)

Instructions regarding War Diaries and Intelligence Summaries are contained in F. S. Regs., Part II. and the Staff Manual respectively. Title pages will be prepared in manuscript.

Place	Date	Hour	Summary of Events and Information	Remarks and references to Appendices
Soignies	28.		Gymkhana Sports Held. Man available strength officers 40 o.r.s rank	
	29.		Gave employer embarking apparatus on pontoons for Aeroplastic Sports.	
	30.		Gave employer repacking apparatus on pontoons.	
	31.		Testing Sign Lamps.	

Capt. Bloore. R.E.
O/C 413 Ky Coy Inld Wtrwys R.E.

www.ingramcontent.com/pod-product-compliance
Lightning Source LLC
Chambersburg PA
CBHW081453160426
43193CB00013B/2465